An
Early History
of
Red Lodge, Montana

by Bruce H. Blevins

Proseyr Publishing
Red Lodge, MT   U.S.A.

Copyright ©2016 Bruce H. Blevins

All rights reserved. No part of this publication may be reproduced, transmitted, or stored in a retrieval system, in any form or by any means, to include: photocopying, electronic, mechanical, recording, or otherwise; without the prior written permission of the author.

An Early History of Red Lodge, Montana
By Bruce H. Blevins

Body copy set in Book Antiqua
Headings set in Myriad Pro

Second Edition
ISBN 978-1-945110-01-6

Proseyr Publishing
PO Box 1630, Red Lodge, MT 59068
www.proseyr.com

An Early History of Red Lodge, Montana

Contents

Preface 3
Chapter 1: Before The Town 5
Chapter 2: Red Lodge Established 11
Chapter 3: Boom Times 15
Chapter 3: The Decline 25
Chapter 4: Changing Character 27
Chapter 5: Place Names 31
Sources 35
Further Information 36
About the Author 37

Bruce H. Blevins

Preface

A short history of Red Lodge, Montana, and vicinity is provided in An Early History of Red Lodge, Montana. This project was started to create a concise history for this intriguing town. Many early histories of Montana include some historical information about the area but they are not books to be read to catch a more fundamental story of Red Lodge. The 1979 Red Lodge, Saga of a Western Area, written by Shirley Zupan and Harry J. Owens for the Carbon County Historical Society, has the most comprehensive and substantial information about the town and is generally organized around specific events, individuals and families.

An Early History of Red Lodge, Montana is a basic narrative emphasizing the early years of Red Lodge and vicinity to 1940 with limited information provided for the years thereafter. Many of the histories have different rendering on some of the events and facts, sometimes apparently caused by simple editing errors. The research for this book tries to track down those differences and use those believed to be most probable. Although any history will contain biases because of the sources used and the author's interpretations. I will use current names for the town and geographic features in the basic account and cover alternate naming of significance in the last chapter. The hope is that this rendition will provide information of interest to both residents and visitors and encourage further exploration.

This second and revised edition includes editing updates, improved explanations and additional illustrations.

Bruce H. Blevins

Center section of the town of Red Lodge.

Chapter 1: Before The Town

The valley that Red Lodge, Montana, now calls home had a less dramatic early history of activity compared to that of some other territories of the early West. The location was not along a well-traveled path in the early history of the West nor an area with precious metals. This would be compensated by the distinctive mountains and valleys that comprise the territory around Red Lodge, for they would eventually lead to its development.

The current geology of the Red Lodge area is dominated by the forces of mountain-building uplifting, volcanic activity, ice ages, water and wind. This has left the territory with the Absaroka-Beartooth Wilderness, a large expanse of mountains that includes seventy-seven named peaks and many more unnamed peaks rising more than two miles in altitude above sea level and are the highest mountains in Montana. A multitude of streams make it "the best watered area in the State of Montana."

Prehistoric humans most likely visited the area to hunt shortly after the last ice age, which ended about 10,000 years ago. Modern-day Indians started visiting the area during the 1500s and the region was probably first controlled by the Shoshone Indians late in the 1700s. The Blackfeet Indians drove the Shoshone Indians out of the territory by 1800. While the Blackfeet would continue to visit the vicinity to hunt, the Crow Indians became the principal visitors and hunters in the valley beginning in the early 1800s.

The first non-Indians to get close to the valley were Captain William Clark and his party during the eastward bound explorations of the Lewis and Clark 1804-1806 Corps of Discovery. Captain Clark, returning from the Pacific Ocean, floated down the Yellowstone River, passing a river coming in from the south that he named the Clarks Fork on July 24, 1806, of which Rock Creek is a tributary beginning twelve miles upstream and flowing through Red Lodge. The resulting 1814 Lewis and Clark map is the earliest published map depicting any detail of the rivers and mountains of this region.

Some early histories reported that the brothers Louis-Joseph and François Verendrye from French Canada visited the Yellowstone River area in 1743. Current historians generally leave the Verendrye brothers' excursions far short of the region, listing their farthest travels west as no further than east of the Big Horn Mountains in what is now eastern Wyoming.

Portion of 1814 Lewis and Clark map showing the area around Red Lodge. "Ap-sah-soo-ha R" is the current Rock Creek at its mouth and then Red Lodge Creek upstream.

George Drouillard, a hunter with the Missouri Fur Company, and previously a member of the Lewis and Clark expedition, mapped a Crow Indian winter camp at the junction of Clarks Fork and Rock Creek in 1807. It is also reported that he visited the Beartooth Mountains. With Drouillard's mapping and reporting in 1808, he may have been the first non-Indian to visit the site of Red Lodge. There was no recorded fur hunting from 1812 to the mid-1820s in the Rocky Mountains because the war of 1812 stopped shipments of furs to England.

Members of the Rocky Mountain Fur Company may have visited Rock Creek in late 1829 after being scattered by Blackfeet Indians while on the northern edge of what is now Yellowstone National Park. The members, who became prominent men of the era, included William Sublette, Jedediah Smith, David Jackson, Joe Meek, and Jim Bridger, reunited on the Shoshone River near present-day Cody, Wyoming.

The first firmly documented non-Indian visit to what is now Rock Creek Valley was beaver-fur hunters for the American Fur Company. Under Jim Bridger's direction, a fur hunting party including Osborne Russell visited Rock Creek on September 7, 1936, on their way to a gathering of fur hunters at the junction of the Clarks Fork and Yellowstone Rivers. After the reunion, seven fur trappers, including Osborne Russell, traveled back to an area probably five to seven miles north of the site of present-day Red Lodge to set beaver traps on Rock Creek on September 19, 1836. They remained in the valley until September 28, during which time several Crow Indians visited with them.

The next recorded visit to the valley was again by Osborne Russell and other hunters of the American Fur Company from April 14 to May 1, 1837. From April 14 to 23, they stayed in the area near what is now the town of Roberts thirteen miles north of Red Lodge. They could go no further south towards Red Lodge to set beaver traps because of snow and ice on Rock Creek until April 24.

From a cave camp site near present day Roberts they "made great havoc among the Buffaloe" in Rock Creek Valley. Then from April 24 to the end of April 1837, some of the hunters set beaver traps around what is now the Red Lodge town site. American Fur Company employees Osborne Russell, William Allen, John Greenberry (an Englishman), and John Conn returned on October 11, 1837, and encamped in the mountains above Rock Creek until October 27. This is the first documented case of non-Indians settling, even if just for a short while, in or above the Red Lodge vicinity. During this time Russell and Allen took a two-day excursion down to the mouth of Rock Creek and back and were "among Buffaloe all day."

With the change of fashion from fur to silk hats, the beaver fur trade declined rapidly and little trapping occurred after 1843. Recorded visits to the area ceased for the next seventeen years.

Vignette from 1868 map depicting eastern view of a Indian buffalo hunt.

A United States treaty signed on September 17, 1851 gave a large part of the Yellowstone River watershed to the Crow Indians. This included all of the area around present-day Red Lodge.

The next documented visit to the area was the Lieutenant Henry E. Maynadier survey party under the direction of Captain William Raynolds as part of the United States Army Survey of the West. Maynadier crossed Rock Creek on June 19, 1860, near present-day Boyd which is about twenty-one miles north of Red Lodge.

In 1866 two gold-seeking parties visited Rock Creek Valley. In the spring James Stuart led 75 men through the area going from

Bozeman, Montana, to northern Wyoming. In July Jeff Standifer, also from Bozeman, led about 100 men into Rock Creek and beyond. Neither party found gold in the Rock Creek Valley. However, rich deposits of coal were found in the valley in 1866. In 1870 gold was discovered near present-day Cooke City, Montana, just outside of the northeast corner of what would become Yellowstone National Park two years later. The discovery of gold near Cooke City would be a major force in opening up the upper Rock Creek Valley to settlement. Because the territory around Cooke City as well as all of Rock Creek was still part of the Crow Indian Reservation, gold mining was illegal and therefore the gold claims were invalid and they were worked irregularly. In 1876 the miners used an old Indian trail over the Beartooth Mountains for the first recorded time to go from Cooke City to Rock Creek.

In 1881 the United State Army created a stage and freight road from Billings, Montana, to Meeteetse, Wyoming, going along Rock Creek to present-day Red Lodge before skirting the mountains to the east into Wyoming.

Bruce H. Blevins

Chapter 2: Red Lodge Established

Because of the precious metal potential the United States made a treaty with the Crow Indians in 1880, removing a small strip of land that included Cooke City and to about six miles north of the future site of Red Lodge from their reservation. The treaty officially opened the area to settlement and mining on April 11, 1882. This enabled gold miners to work legally near Cooke City and settlers to move into the area around what would become Red Lodge. Limited coal mining was initiated during this time in what would eventually become known as the Red Lodge coal field.

Red Lodge was established as a stage stop on the route between Billings, Montana, and Meeteetse, Wyoming, in early 1883. That same year a trail was blazed over the Beartooth Mountains from Cooke City to Red Lodge by the Van Dyke family. This trail has been called the Van Dyke Trail and the Slickrock Trail. Another trail up Mount Maurice to Cooke City was established and called the Black & White Trail. As a result of the routes to Cooke City and those to Meeteetse and Cody, Wyoming, Red Lodge became an important stop for stage and pack-animals freight train shipments carrying people and supplies from the Yellowstone River boat docks and then the railroad stations near Billings, Montana.

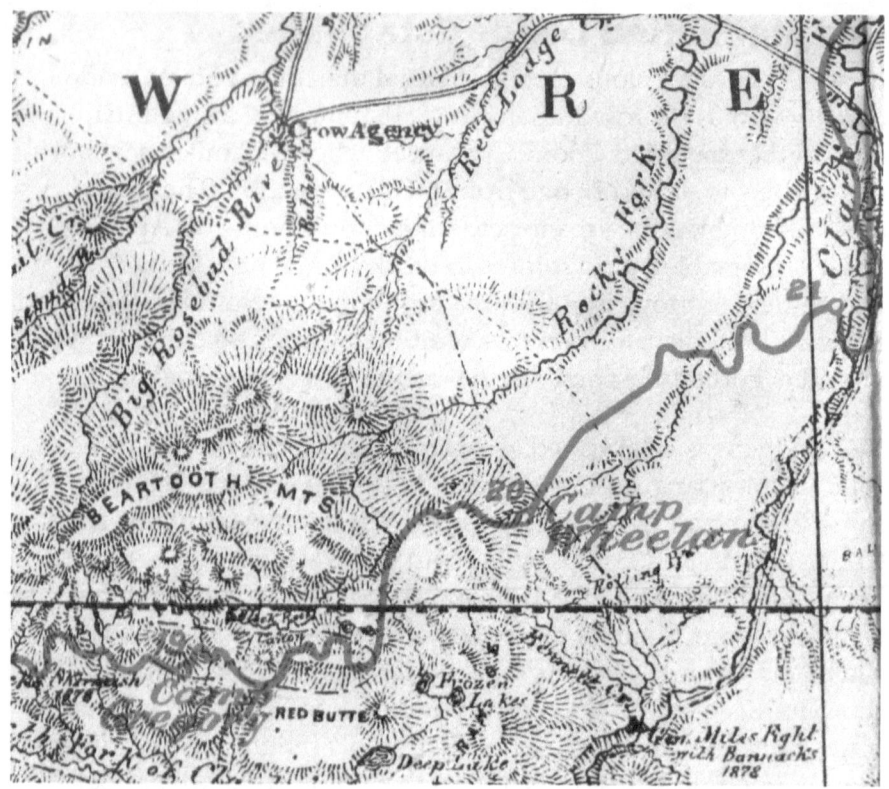

Portion of 1882 Map of General Sheridan's route through the area. Illustrates the knowledge of the terrain as of 1882, just as the territory was being opened for settlement.

On December 9, 1884, a Post Office named "Red Lodge" was granted to Red Lodge, which at that time was in Gallatin County. Red Lodge was now officially on the map. In 1886 James "Yankee Jim" George interested M. M. Black, Walker Cooper, and others of Bozeman, Montana, in the coal mining at Red Lodge. They started the Rocky Fork Coal Company, and major mines were opened in 1887 with pack-animal freight train shipments to Billings. Rocky Fork was an early name for Rock Creek.

In 1888 the first merchants opened stores and the first newspaper, the Red Lodge Picket, commenced publication.

An Early History of Red Lodge, Montana

Portion of 1884 W & A. K. Johnson map of Wyoming, Idaho, Montana & Dakota illustrates Red Lodge in the year the Post Office was created and before the railroad was established.

Meanwhile, the Northern Pacific Railroad was given a grant for a transcontinental railroad across Montana in 1870 which was completed to the Pacific Coast in 1883. In 1886 organizers not associated with the Northern Pacific Railroad started the Rocky Fork and Cooke City Railway and proposed a line that would extend from the Northern Pacific Railroad at Billings to Red Lodge and then on to Cooke City. The purpose was to exploit the Red Lodge coal field and the Cooke City gold, neither of which could be real money making propositions without good transportation. Surveys began in April 1887 and grading was under way by October of that year. Just as the railroad bed was about to be complete to Red Lodge, the company ran out of money and the work stopped. In August 1888, another company, also not associated with the Northern Pacific Railroad, was formed as the Billings, Clark's Fork and Cooke City Railroad. This railroad aspired to exploit the Red Lodge coal field by approaching from the other side of Bearcreek pass east of Red Lodge and then to access the gold claims near Cooke City. They planned to have the line completed to Cooke City by July 1889 — a wild dream. Alarmed by all this competition, parties associated with the Northern Pacific Railroad purchased the defunct Rocky Fork and Cooke City Railway and extended the Northern Pacific route to Red Lodge by April 1889.

Bruce H. Blevins

*Red Lodge railroad station built in 1889,
now enlarged and restored as an art gallery*

When the railroad's first shipment of coal left Red Lodge on June 17, 1889, the boom began. With the rest of Rock Creek Valley being ceded by the Crow Indians on October 15, 1892, the growth of the whole region started and increased the economic well-being and profile of Red Lodge.

Chapter 3: Boom Times

The arrival of the railroad in 1889 brought the coal mining into a rapid expansion and a major operation. The Rocky Fork Coal Company was the biggest enterprise, but several other smaller companies also exploited the coal field at Red Lodge which was stated to be sub-bituminous coal "unequaled in the west" and whose volume was estimated to fill a solid block one mile square and 1,300 feet high. The coal was used by the Northern Pacific Railroad in their steam locomotives, in smelters and mills, and for domestic purposes. The coal was being burned from the Mississippi River to the Pacific Ocean.

The year 1889 brought rapid growth to Red Lodge with the completion of the railroad. A sawmill south of town was started to provide timber for the mines; it also supplied lumber for house and store construction. The Rocky Fork Town and Electric Company obtained title to the land north of what is now 16th Street and platted the town. At this time 16th Street was the major business district. The electricity was needed in the mines but had the added benefit of making the town one of the best electric-served towns for its size and times.

The first mercantile established opened this same year and the first one-room, one-teacher school was started in September. By the end of 1889 the town had about 400 people and the 1890 census listed Red Lodge with 624 people.

Buildings on 16th Street, which was the main Red Lodge business district to the mid-1890s.

With the opening up of the rest of the Rock Creek Valley in 1892 from the previous Crow Indian reservation land, the area north of Red Lodge had a surge of settlers and major agriculture development began. In 1892 a petition was started to incorporate the town of Red Lodge and the accompanied census listed 1,180 people.

Early in 1894 a majority of the people wanted to remain part of Park County but during the winter of 1894–1895 a desire to become an independent county division became the rage. Just before the bill was introduced into the Montana Legislature a committee of citizens recommended the name Carbon County be used, since the Red Lodge area was then the largest producer of coal in the state. The bill easily passed the Montana House but it was a tie vote in the Montana Senate. The Lieutenant Governor made the deciding vote in favor of the bill which created Carbon County, at one time called the "Gem of the Mountains," with Red Lodge as the County Seat.

In 1898 the Northern Pacific Railroad decided to shift its coal operations base from Bozeman, Montana, to the richer coal veins at Red Lodge. The Northwestern Improvement Company was formed by the Northern Pacific Railroad to handle its coal mining activities. The Northwestern Improvement Company led the expansion of the coal field and obtained control of the Rocky Fork Coal Company. The major mine in the area was the Northwestern Improvement Company's East Side Mine, across Rock Creek from the town. In 1907 the West Side Mine, also called the Sunset Mine, was started by the Northwestern Improvement Company. Over 12,000 coal car loads left via the rails with output from the Red Lodge coal field in 1910. That was about four million dollars of coal in 1910 which is around 100 million dollars in today's dollars.

The remnants of the East Side Mine building

The opening up of the coal mining activity with the completion of the railroad in 1889 and the moving of the Northern Pacific coal operations to Red Lodge in 1898 brought a large influx of mine workers. The vast majority of these miners were immigrants. By 1910 half of Red Lodge's nearly 5,000 population were immigrants. While most immigrants were from Eastern Europe and the largest ethnic group was made up of over 1,000 people from Finland, the countries of origin included: Finland, countries that became Yugoslavia after World War I (principally Servia,

Bruce H. Blevins

Bosina, Croatia and Slavonia, and Montenegro), Italy, Germany, Austria-Hungary, Norway, Sweden, Ireland, Wales, Scotland, Poland, and Russia.

Because the Rocky Fork Coal Company and then the Northwestern Improvement Company did not enforce the rule that miners had to live in company provided housing, Red Lodge took on a distinct feel of not being a company town and one of having a great pride in its individual cultures. The ethnic distinctions were enhanced by the settlement of the immigrants into their own enclaves within the town.

From 1888 to the mid 1890s the business district of Red Lodge was along 16th Street. By 1896 the business district shifted to what is now Broadway. The citizens voted for a water works in 1899 with centralized water being available by October 1901. In July 1900, an organized fire fighting force was started being spurred on by a March 23, 1900, business center fire.

By 1906 the town consisted of 4,000 people with the major named sections being: Business District, Old Town (the old business district along 16th Street), Finn Town, Little Italy, Austrians living between 16th and 17th streets, the Yugoslavians near the old business district, and the more well off in Hi-Bug Town which was made up of mostly citizens born in the United States.

In the 1910 census the town had 4,860 people and ranked 10th among Montana cities.

See page 19 for a concept map of Red Lodge from around 1910.

At the end of 1906, the organized churches were: Congregational Church started in 1890, Calvary Episcopal started in 1890, Finnish Evangelical Lutheran, Methodist Episcopal started in 1891, St Agnes Catholic started in 1893 and the Adventists who "do not hold regular weekly services." Eight secret societies also existed: Carbon County Lodge A.O.U., Bear Tooth Lodge B.P.O.E., Brindle

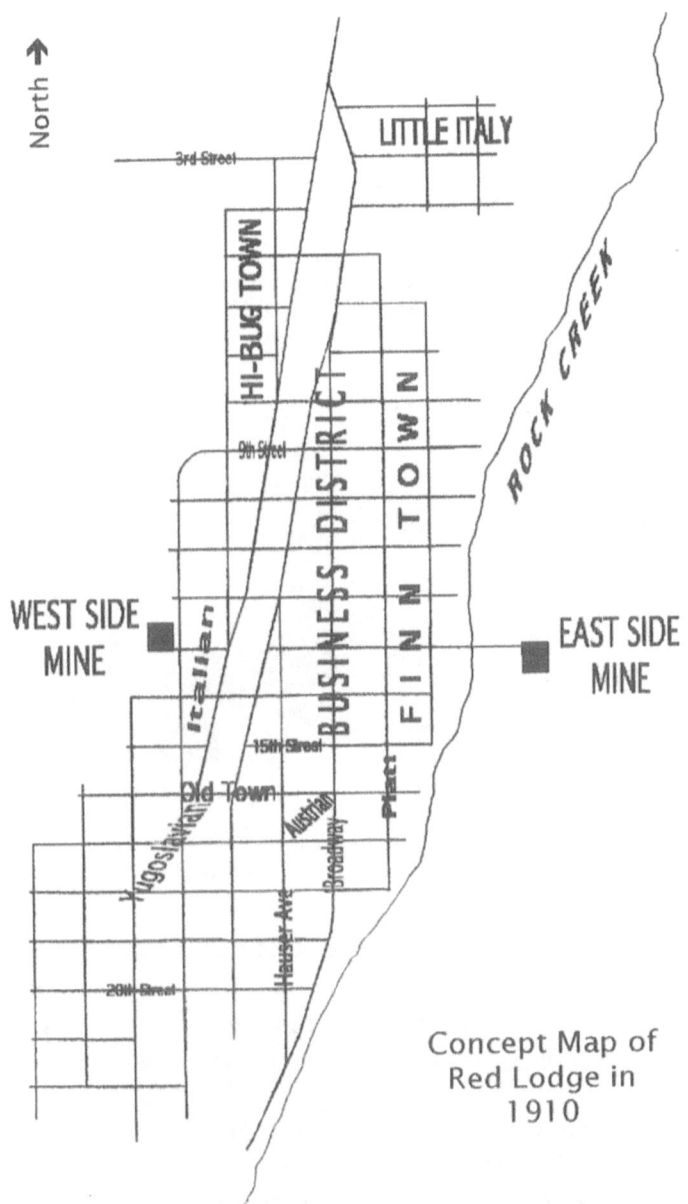

Concept Map of Red Lodge in 1910

Court Catholic Order of Foresters, Red Lodge Aerie F.O.E., Garfield Lodge I.O.O.F., Star of the West Lodge A.F. & A.M., Summit Camp W.O.W. and Red Lodge Cabin Fraternal Order of Mountaineers.

Restored 1903 Hi-Bug Town house.

By 1906 the Rock Creek Valley had a wide variety of agriculture-based products including cattle, sheep, alfalfa, timothy, wheat, barley, oats, flax, clover, potatoes, small fruits, honey, dairy operations, vegetables, and thoroughbred draft horse breeding.

In 1906 the Yellowstone Park Railroad Company completed a rail line from Bridger, Montana, to Bearcreek and Washoe, seven and three miles east of Red Lodge respectively. This enabled better transportation access to the eastern portion of the Red Lodge coal field. Bearcreek had been established in 1905 and Washoe in

Restored 1910 Finn Town house.

1906 as a result of the desire to more efficiently work the eastern portion of the coal field. The Bearcreek Post Office was established in 1906 and the Washoe Post Office in 1907. With the completion of the railroad to Bearcreek and Washoe, major production from the coal field was conducted near these towns. Many miners commuted from Red Lodge and the major business center remained Red Lodge. In 1910 the Bearcreek census was 302 with no census given for Washoe in the available sources.

In 1907 Red Lodge's future looked bright as a major city in Montana. A branch line of the railroad from Bearcreek, just east of Red Lodge, planned to be completed to Cooke City by 1908 which would finally open up the gold claims — the dream continues. Petroleum fields had been discovered east of Red Lodge. The Beartooth Mountains contained an "everlasting" supply of water and timber with sculpture, limestone, marble and iron in abundance.

A 1907 history stated "The county of Carbon has a brilliant future assured. No county in the state has so many and varied resources. It has the best defined and best developed beds of high grade semi-bituminous coal west of the Missouri River, many fertile valleys where crop failures are unknown and the yield is always surprising large, a good home market for all produce, and, above all, a good healthful and invigorating climate and industrious and law abiding citizens." The same history reported that the Signal Service observers, presumably in 1906–1907, stated that "this section of Montana has more sunshine than any section of country in the world."

However, not all was positive during this era, with two mine disasters that claimed lives. The first was in the East Side Mine on June 6, 1906, claiming seven or eight would-be rescuers (all the histories say eight men died; the history published in 1907 that lists the men's names states "8" but only gave seven names). The second disaster during this period was also in the East Side Mine on November 2, 1908, claiming nine men.

From 1910 to 1917 Red Lodge and vicinity maintained a slow but steady growth, although the predicted railroad to Cooke City and the fortunes one hoped that would bring did not materialize.

Bruce H. Blevins

Chapter 3: The Decline

In 1918 a decline in the Red Lodge prospects began to show. Red Lodge population had dropped to 4,515 in 1920 from a probable high of near 5,500 a few years before and its ranking went from 10th to 13th among Montana cities. Red Lodge still looked prosperous with three banks, eight grocery stores, ten clothing stores, two hospitals, a theater, and a Carnegie Library. Nearby Bearcreek and Washoe populations were 744 and 250 in the same 1920 census.

Miner strikes and threatened strikes were making the supply of coal from the Red Lodge field less dependable. Labor costs were rising. As a result, in the early 1920s the Northern Pacific Railroad began to explore strip mining of coal in southeastern Montana. In 1924 the Northern Pacific Railroad began open surface mining around Colstrip, Montana, with far cheaper labor costs and easier and safer production techniques than underground tunneling. In 1926 the Northwestern Improvement Company closed the West Side Mine. In the 1930 census Red Lodge's population had dropped to 3,026, Bearcreek's population had dropped to 472 and Washoe's population had risen slightly to 295. The Northwestern Improvement Company closed the East Side Mine in 1932.

By the early 1940s the demand for coal fell sharply as railroads increasingly converted to diesel locomotives and homes and business turned to fuel oil and natural gas for heating. During World War II there was a brief opening of the Red Loge coal field at the Smith Mine near Bearcreek but a mine explosion in 1943 killed 74 miners and signaled the end for any significant coal mining operations in the area to this day.

Smith Mine #3 as it appears today, after the train tracks were removed

The chrome deposits that had been discovered earlier, where opened briefly during World War II on a nonprofit basis with the help of the federal government. The chrome was used in iron and steel products to prevent rust. The road to Hell Roaring Plateau south of Red Lodge and a reduction mill on the East Bench above the site of the old East Side Mine were built during this period to extract the chrome. At the end of World War II, chrome production stopped and mining ceased to be an economic factor for Red Lodge.

Remains of the Chrome Reduction works above the East Side Mine.

Chapter 4: Changing Character

In the 1920s, coincident with the decline in mining, tourist-related activities started with the increased availability of cars. While these activities would never replace the economic impact of the coal mines, they would eventually alter the character of the town. Tourist camps began development in the 1920s and by the 1930s and 1940s the resorts and a rodeo were bringing visitors into Red Lodge in larger and larger numbers. A ski operation was started at Willow Creek (along present-day Grizzly Peak) in 1941.

The most dramatic development in the tourist trade of the 1930s and 1940s was the construction and opening of the Red Lodge–Cooke City Highway, now named the Beartooth Highway. Efforts to get a road built began as early at 1919. A bill called the Park Approach Act passed Congress, and was signed by the President on January 31, 1931. Although the highway to Cooke City was not specifically mentioned, it was the only proposed road that could meet all the conditions of the bill. A total of three million dollars was appropriated over two years.

Construction began in 1931 and the road was officially opened on June 14, 1936, at a cost of two and a half million dollars. A 1936 Red Loge advertising brochure named "Over the Top via Red Lodge–Cooke City HIGHway to and from Yellowstone Park" saying America's new Scenic Highway is "the safest highway in any mountain region climbing from 6000 feet in Rock Creek Canyon and zigzagging upwards 24 miles with a grade of 5½ percent until the top plateau is reached at 11,000 feet."

The original names of the various switchbacks have largely disappeared from use but the 1939 Montana State Guide Book lists the following in order of ascent: Primal Switchback, Big Full turn, Deadwood Switchback, Wyoming Rock Turn, Mae West Curve and Frozen Man's Curve.

Bruce H. Blevins

Montana Switchbacks of the Beartooth Highway climbing out of Rock Creek Valley

The end of World War II brought an even larger tourist trade with the growing economy, vehicle purchases and more leisure time.

The 1950 census listed Red Lodge's population as 2,730, ranking if 23rd among Montana cities. Beginning in the 1950s, the citizens of Red Lodge did many things to provide progress for the town and move it forward to today's environment. A community building effort began which had some successes, like the civic center and new hospital.

Tourist trade was promoted and increased by the annual Festival of Nations, which began in 1950; the Home of Champions Rodeo, designated in 1953; the Grizzly Peak Ski Run (now called Red Lodge Mountain), which opened in 1960; and the music festival, which started in 1963. In 1989 the Red Lodge–Cooke City Highway was designated on the National Scenic Byways. Major portions of the Absarokee Forest Reserve that was set aside by proclamation by President Roosevelt in 1902, was designated the Absaroka-Beartooth Wilderness in 1978.

In the 1990 census Red Lodge is listed with 1,950 people, ranking it 33rd among Montana cities. The coal mines are no longer operational and the railroad tracks have been removed from both Red Lodge and Bearcreek-Washoe localities. Today agriculture, tourism, and county government are the main livelihood of Red Lodge and vicinity. The 2010 census has Red Lodge growing to 2,125 people and ranking moved up to 31st with the increased tourist trade.

Bruce H. Blevins

Portion of 1867 Raynolds map from 1860 survey by Lt. Maynadier illustrating Rocky Fork.

Portion of 1878 Mitchell map of Colorado, Wyoming, Dakota, Montana illustrating Rock Creek.

Chapter 5: Place Names

Based upon information he obtained from the Indians, Captain William Clark of the Lewis and Clark expedition named a tributary of the Clarks Fork the "Ap sah soo ha" River. The 1814 Lewis and Clark map (illustrated in Chapter 1) carries the name upstream along what is now Red Lodge Creek to the west of Rock Creek, leaving the current Rock Creek a tributary of Red Lodge Creek. Eventually Red Lodge Creek became a tributary of Rock Creek, which flows through Red Lodge. The fur trappers called Rock Creek "Rocky Fork" starting at least as early as 1836.

Lieutenant Maynadier's crew surveyed the lower potion of Rock Creek for the Captain Raynolds Survey of the West and labeled the stream Rocky Fork on their 1860 map published in 1867. The United States Land Office map maker called it Rock Creek starting in 1869. The 1878 Mitchell map is one of the earliest commercial maps to use Rock Creek. Rocky Fork and Rock Creek were used on maps interchangeably from 1872 to 1897 with Rock Creek becoming the standard after 1897. The naming based upon rocks is an obvious choice along many portions of the river.

Red Lodge

The origin of the name "Red Lodge" has been lost to history. Explanations include (a) there was a Crow Indian gathering near the present-day town site and, because the meat spoiled, the Indians called the area Bad Lodge with misinterpretation changing Bad to Red, (b) the Crow Indians had one or more lodges (teepees) colored by red clay near the future town site, (c) at one time there were many Crow Indian "red man's" lodges in the area of what is now the town site and the shortened term Red Lodge developed and d) on the side of a mountain west of Red Lodge reddish colored rocks look like an Indian lodge from a distance, resulting in the name Red Lodge Creek. Because Red Lodge Creek is well to the west of the town of Red Lodge, the name "Red Lodge" may have had nothing to do with the Rock Creek vicinity.

Red Lodge, with an altitude listed at 5,555 feet, was officially named in 1884 with the assignment of the Post Office. The town of Red Lodge first appears on the 1884 map illustrated in Chapter 2.

Rocky Fork was also a name used for the settlement by some based upon the miners claims, the name of the railroad spur that started in 1886, and the platting of the town by the Rocky Fork Town and Electric Company in 1889. Rocky Fork did not make any known published maps for the name of the settlement. Villard was temporary chosen as the town's name to replace Red Lodge in 1889 when the railroad reached town. This was done to honor Henry Villard who was president of the Northern Pacific Railroad when the transcontinental route was completed in 1883. Although Villard helped in getting the spur line to Red Lodge, by 1889 he had been out of office as president of the railroad for five years and he declined the honor of having the town named after him. Although the name immediately reverted to Red Lodge, for several years the maps carried Villard and then "Villard or Red Lodge" before Red Lodge once again became the standard.

An Early History of Red Lodge, Montana

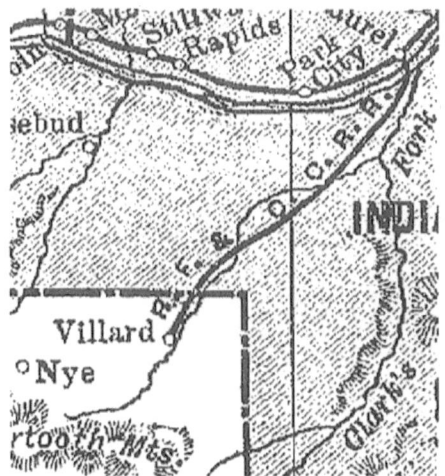

Portion of 1897 Peerless Atlas map of Montana illustrating Villard for Red Lodge town name and the Rocky Fork & Cooke City Rail Road.

Red Lodge is the sole name used for the settlement beginning in 1900. The present Carbon County boundaries were fixed in 1913 when Stillwater County was created from parts of Carbon and other surrounding counties.

Portion of 1921 L. L. Poates map of Montana, illustrating Red Lodge and Carbon County.

Bruce H. Blevins

Sources

The principal sources used for the information in *An Early History of Red Lodge, Montana* were:

An Illustrated History of the Yellowstone Valley, Western Historical Publishing Company, undated but written in 1907

Journal of a Trapper, Nine years in the Rocky Mountains 1834-1843, L. A. York, 1914

Montana - Its Story and Biography under the Supervision of Tom Stout, The American Historical Society, 1921

History of Montana by Helen Fitzgerald Sanders, The Lewis Publishing Company, 1913

A History of Montana, Merrill G. Burlingame, K. Roaa Toole, Lewis Historical Publishing Company, 1957

Montana: A State Guide Book, Federal Writer's Project of the Work Projects Administration, Hasting House Publishers, 1939

Beartooth Highway Experiences, Bruce H. Blevins, WIM Marketing, 2003

Original maps, cited and others, from 1814 to 1921 and current United States Geological Survey maps

Bruce H. Blevins

Further Information

Recommended reading for further information about the vicinity:

Red Lodge, Saga of a Western Area, Shirley Zupan and Harry J. Owens, Carbon County Historical Society, 1979, and *The Darkest Hour: A Comprehensive Account of the Smith Mine Disaster of 1943*, Fay Kuhlman and Gary D. Robson, will provide many interesting stories.

Beartooth Country by Bob Anderson, Montana Magazine and American & World Geographic Publishing, 1994, and *The Beartooth Highway* by H. L. James, Montana Bureau of Mines and Geology, 1995, provide many enjoyable related facts.

About the Author

Bruce Blevins was born in Powell, Wyoming, and graduated from Dubois, Wyoming, high school in 1965. After graduating from Montana State University with a degree in Mathematics, Bruce went to work as a civilian employee with the National Security Agency in Maryland. The end of the cold war presented an opportunity to take early retirement which Bruce did, moving to the Powell-Cody-Red Lodge area in 1997.

Bruce's fun is historic research which has resulted in eleven regional history books. Most of his book involve maps, map histories or surveying. This interest was fueled by surveying work with the US Geological Survey and Bureau of Public Road during college summers. The collecting of antique maps added the history flavor.

Other books still available include:

- *Beartooth Highway Experiences*

- *Mapping Yellowstone, A History of the Mapping of Yellowstone National Park*

- *Absaroka Mountains 1893 and 1897, Jaggar's Diaries and Photographs*

- *Wyoming Montana Border, They followed the 45th 1879-1880*

- *Tinker's Bighorn Canyon* - ebook only

Bruce H. Blevins

www.ingramcontent.com/pod-product-compliance
Lightning Source LLC
Chambersburg PA
CBHW021453080526
44588CB00009B/837